AUDIO
ACCESS
INCLUDED

LAYBACK+

d • Pitch • Balance • Loop

VIOLIN

WEST SIDE STORY®

T0079947

Based on a conception of Jerome Robbins

Book by

Arthur Laurents

Music by

Leonard Bernstein®

Lyrics by

Stephen Sondheim

Entire Original Production

Directed and Choreographed by

Jerome Robbins

ISBN 978-1-4234-5830-2

To access companion recorded audio, visit:
www.halleonard.com/mylibrary

Enter Code
4394-5517-3588-1377

LEONARD
BERNSTEIN
Music Publishing
Company LLC

BOOSEY & HAWKES

DISTRIBUTED BY

HAL•LEONARD®

Visit Hal Leonard Online at
www.halleonard.com

World headquarters, contact:
Hal Leonard
7777 West Bluemound Road
Milwaukee, WI 53213
Email: info@halleonard.com

In Europe, contact:
Hal Leonard Europe Limited
42 Wigmore Street
Marylebone, London, W1U 2RN
Email: info@halleonardeurope.com

In Australia, contact:
Hal Leonard Australia Pty. Ltd.
4 Lentara Court
Cheltenham, Victoria, 3192 Australia
Email: info@halleonard.com.au

CONTENTS

3   America

4   Cool

5   I Feel Pretty

6   I Have a Love

7   Jet Song

8   Maria

9   One Hand, One Heart

10   Something's Coming

12   Somewhere

13   Tonight

The price of this publication includes access to companion recorded audio online, for download or streaming, using the unique code found on the title page. Visit **www.halleonard.com/mylibrary** and enter the access code.

A melody cue is included on the right channel only which may be adjusted up or down to hear the accompaniment or full version.

◆ AMERICA

VIOLIN

Lyrics by STEPHEN SONDHEIM
Music by LEONARD BERNSTEIN

◆ 2 COOL

VIOLIN

Lyrics by STEPHEN SONDHEIM
Music by LEONARD BERNSTEIN

❸ I FEEL PRETTY

Violin

Lyrics by STEPHEN SONDHEIM
Music by LEONARD BERNSTEIN

◆4 I HAVE A LOVE

VIOLIN

Lyrics by STEPHEN SONDHEIM
Music by LEONARD BERNSTEIN

◆ JET SONG

VIOLIN

Lyrics by STEPHEN SONDHEIM
Music by LEONARD BERNSTEIN

 MARIA

VIOLIN

Lyrics by STEPHEN SONDHEIM
Music by LEONARD BERNSTEIN

◆ ONE HAND, ONE HEART

Violin

Lyrics by STEPHEN SONDHEIM
Music by LEONARD BERNSTEIN

◆ SOMETHING'S COMING

VIOLIN

Lyrics by STEPHEN SONDHEIM
Music by LEONARD BERNSTEIN

⟨9⟩ SOMEWHERE

VIOLIN

Lyrics by STEPHEN SONDHEIM
Music by LEONARD BERNSTEIN

◆10 TONIGHT

VIOLIN

Lyrics by STEPHEN SONDHEIM
Music by LEONARD BERNSTEIN